Our Church

Our Church

Text by Graham English

Illustrated by Marjory Gardner

THE LITURGICAL PRESS
Collegeville, Minnesota

I'M MARY,
I AM TEN YEARS OLD AND I'M A CATHOLIC.

This is my church. I became a Catholic when I was
baptised and if you are baptised it's your church, too.
I live in St Mary's parish. Our parish is new, Mum says.
Really it's twelve years old which doesn't seem new to me.
Here is a picture of some of the other people in our parish.
Their names are underneath so you can tell who they are.
I live with Mum and Dad and my sister Geraldine. She's
called after our aunty. Mum says that Geraldine is a kind
of Catholic name. When my mother was little, nearly all
Catholics had saints' names either for their first or second
name. Lots of them still do. My second name is Josephine.
Sometimes when we are watching television at Gran's
place she hears a name and then she says 'Now that sounds
like a Catholic name'.
I go to school at St Mary's school. (It's not called after
me!) My teacher is Miss Ravanello.
This is a drawing of Miss Ravanello. She's good at sport
and plays netball in a team called the Galloping Girls.
That seems a funny name to me.

MY NAME IS NINA AND I LIVE WITH MY FAMILY AND MOTHER AND MY TWO SISTERS CORIE AND JACINTA.

My mother and father were born in the Philippines but now we live in Australia. I like it here. My dad gets us all to say the rosary with him every night after tea. Sometimes we argue because he wants to say the rosary when we want to watch TV. One of Dad's favourite people is Our Lady. One thing that annoys me is my birthday which is on the 16th of March. It always happens in Lent and Dad and Mum say that I have to wait until Easter to have a party. Of course Easter is the most important day for Catholics, even more important than Christmas. But it's hard waiting all through Lent. Dad and Mum tell us stories about the Philippines. Nearly everyone there is a Catholic which is different from Australia.
My mum and dad got married here at St Mary's church but by a Filippino priest. It was the first wedding at St Mary's church.

I'M MAX.
I'M A CATHOLIC

but Mr Spackman who's a friend of my grandfather and who's a bit old like him always calls us tykes. I asked my granddad what that means and he said it's just another way of saying Catholics. 'Is it an insult?' I asked him and he said that it usually isn't . 'There used to be some people in Australia who didn't like Catholics,' he said, 'but these days the different churches get on well. I suppose some people were scared because we were a bit different. I think some of them thought we'd try to make them like us.'
I thought about that. It's strange how some people don't like people who are different. Lucky they don't live in our street because nearly everyone is different. My best friend in the street is Nguen Chin Cap and he's a Buddhist. Helen, Mum's big sister, gave me a crucifix for my first Communion. Chin Cap asked me what it meant and I said that it is Jesus on the cross. The main thing in the Catholic church is that Jesus died on the cross and then rose from the dead on Easter Sunday.

My best friend
Nguen Chin Cap

HELLO. I'M MATTHEW AND I'M A CATHOLIC.

I live with Terry and Jenny who are my new mum and dad. At present I am fostered but soon I will be adopted. My real mother is dead and my father can't look after me. Jenny and Terry had no children and they went to Catholic Adoptions and so here I am. When I first came my social worker Liz talked to me a lot and I had to decide if I wanted to stay and Jenny and Terry had to decide if they wanted me to stay. Sometimes we go and see my other father and he said that later on he'll take me playing golf. I'm looking forward to that. Sometimes I feel really sad that my real mother is dead. Terry and Jenny take me to see her grave sometimes and I take flowers, usually chrysanthemums, because I think they were her favourites. When people die they are with God. I sometimes imagine my mother talking to Jesus. We have a border collie dog called Webster.

My social worker Liz

H I. I'M SHANTI AND I'M A CATHOLIC.

I am glad I live in St Mary's parish because when they built our church they put in wide aisles and no steps so I can get in. Lots of buildings, churches especially, aren't easy for me. They have steps everywhere and there are seats and other things everywhere. My name, Shanti, is an Indian word for peace. My mum and dad like names like that so they called my brother Francis after St Francis from Assisi in Italy. My dad is really good on the guitar and Mum is good on the flute. They're in a bush band and they also play for the music at Mass most Sunday nights. Mum said she learnt the piano and the flute from Sister Isadore at the convent. She also says that her grandfather was Irish and he could play the fiddle and the tin whistle really well. Mum's name is Erin which is a reminder that her family used to be Irish. Maybe some people will think I used to be Indian.

This is Bruna Favera who is my best friend ←

This is a map of my church and the places around about it.

MY NAME IS JASON JOSEPH FARRELL. I'LL BE TEN IN AUGUST AND I'M A CATHOLIC.

My family have lived near here for seven generations. That's about a hundred and thirty years my father says. My nan is not a Catholic. She's a Presbyterian. I asked her about it and she took me down to see her church. It is different from ours even though she's a Christian too. I have Pop's and Nan's wedding photo and also a photo of the church they were married in. Gosh churches looked different in the old days. My nan and pop were married in 1952! My pop told me that when he married Nan his parents weren't very pleased and hers weren't either because they were marrying someone from a different church. I'm glad they got married anyway because I like them.

HELLO, I'M PHILOMENA.

My best friend Emily Carmody calls me Philo but nobody else does. I'm a Catholic and I came to Australia with my family from Sri Lanka. My last name is Fernandes which is not Sri Lankan but Portuguese. When Portuguese Catholics came to Sri Lanka and told the people about Jesus they changed their old names to Portuguese names. Some of my cousins in Sri Lanka have changed their name back but we haven't.

I live with my sister Anatai and my parents. On special days my mother dresses in a sari and my father wears Sri Lankan clothes too. Sometimes Father Barry comes to our place for dinner. He likes hot curries and my mum and dad are really good at cooking them. Mum and Dad go to St Mary's parish and they help run Marriage Encounter. Mum helps Mrs Roncali give out Communion and visit the old people in their houses.

Father Barry christened my sister Anatai.

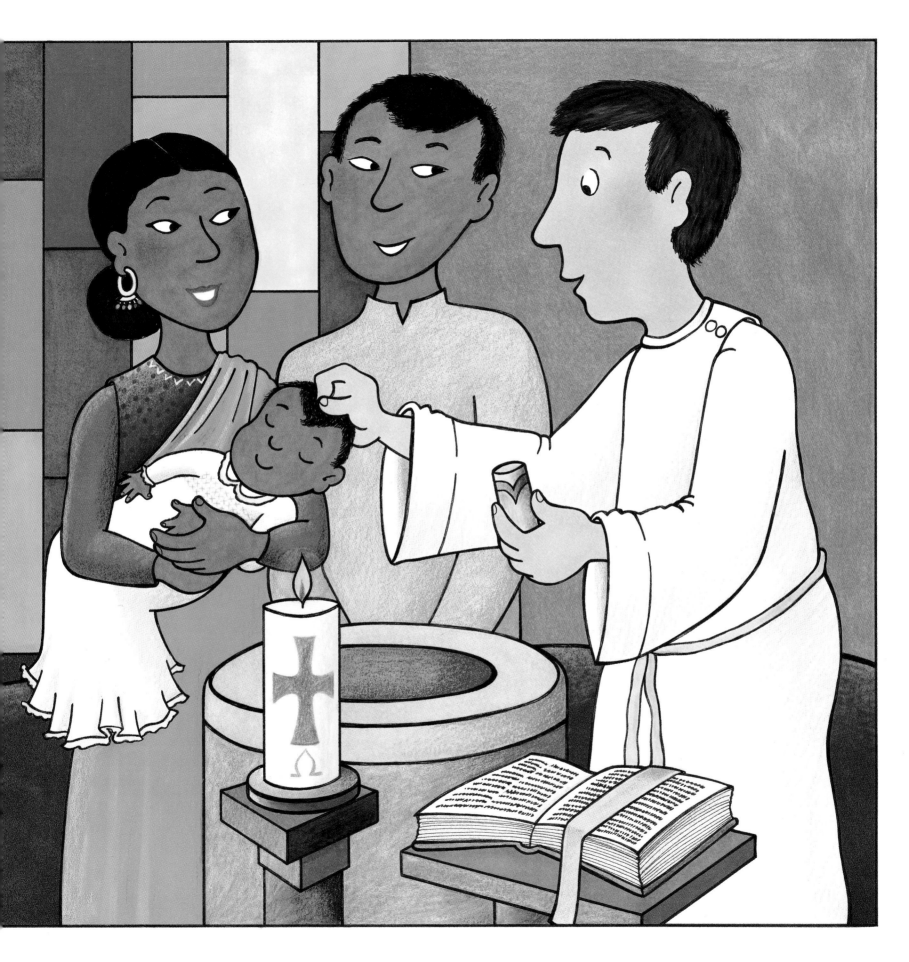

HELLO I'M MICHAEL AND I'M A CATHOLIC.

Our church has been going on for a very long time. I was born in Vietnam where most of the people are not Catholics though lots are. I can't remember Vietnam but my father and mother can. There they used to live near the church and the big bell at the church rang often for Mass and other things so they could tell the time by when the bell rang. We came to Australia in a small boat because we wanted to be free to keep our religion and to live ordinary lives. In Vietnam it was hotter than here and so Mass was held at 5.30 in the morning. And there, too, the church was the main place for people to meet. They had clubs and organisations for people. Some were for saying prayers and helping other people and some were just for fun. I think my mother and father miss Vietnam. I would really like to have my grandparents here and some of my relations. Still I have lots of friends and our church is a good place to meet. We have a cricket team that I am in and my father is the scorer.

This is me playing cricket in St Mary's team.

HELLO THERE. I AM GIOVANNI AND I'M A CATHOLIC.

I'm nine and a half. My best friend Max always calls me Geeves so now everyone does except my dad. I live with my dad and mum and my brother Guiseppe and my sister Bruna. My brother is always called Pippo. My sister Bruna is Shanti Stuart's best friend and so I sometimes push Shanti's wheelchair and help her when she's getting in or out of it. Also I can play the piano accordian and I am practising with Shanti's mum and dad and they said that when I get better I can play with them at Mass on Sunday night. My dad says next thing they'll be dancing in the church and I said they are already and it's called liturgical dancing. Alice Dargan told me that Koori people have been dancing for God for thousands of years so it's about time we did. I told Maria Almeide that and she said, 'So have the people in Spain'. It's surprising the things you find out!

We had a folk mass on the night the bishop came for Confirmation.

HELLO I'M EMMA AND I'M A CATHOLIC.

So is my dad but my mum isn't. She's Uniting Church. I don't go to the Catholic school so Mrs Azzopardi comes to our school to teach us about Jesus and Mary and our church. I really like Mrs Azzopardi. She helped me get ready for my first Communion. Mum often prays with me. She really knows a lot about the Bible. She learnt a lot about it at Sunday School when she was my age. Catholics don't usually have Sunday School. I go to Mass with Dad. Sometimes Mum comes with us and sometimes we go with her to her church. It looks different on the inside. At her church one of the priests is a woman, Rev. Mary McIntosh. Mum says she really likes it when a woman runs the church. Mum has got Dad to go and learn more about the Bible with her and they both read me stories from it. I really like the stories about the Good Samaritan and the one about Ruth. I am going to take Ruth for my Confirmation name.

This is how mum's church looks on the inside. It's a bit different from St. Mary's.

I AM CHRISTINE AND I AM A CATHOLIC.

I live with my mother and father, Nadia my sister and my brothers Joseph, Jawed and Boutros. And my grandma. We call her Sytee which is Arabic. We are Maronite Catholics. Sytee came here from Lebanon with Jidee (that's Arabic for granddad) and us a year ago. But Jidee died just after we came. I was very sad then. Just before Jidee died Father Michael, the Maronite priest, came to our house. We go to the Maronite church on special occasions like the feast of St Charbel. There we can talk in Arabic and hear all the news from Lebanon. We left there because of the war. For a while, when we first came, a special teacher came to my school to teach me English.
My teacher is Mrs Croker and she helped me write properly. It is strange learning a new language and new ways of doing so many things.

Catholics in Australia
We did this graph at school.

The Lebanese flag ←

Buonas Dias Amigos!

I'M MARIA AND I'M A CATHOLIC

and I just said Good-day in Spanish. I have two sisters
Caterina and Pia and two brothers Pedro and Luis and I am
the youngest. There have been Catholics in Spain for
nearly two thousand years. St Paul, who wrote some of the
Bible, went to Spain to tell people about Jesus and then
Spanish people went to lots of countries to tell the people
there. Maybe one day I will be a missionary though I will
be an Australian missionary who can speak Spanish as
well as English. There have been lots of saints in Spain like
St Teresa and St Ignatius and St Francis Xavier. My aunty
told me—she's a nun and knows a whole lot about saints.
When she was little nearly all the teachers in Catholic
schools were nuns. Instead of being called Miss they were
called Sister. And in boys' schools there were brothers.

My Uncle Roger is still in Spain. He's a Brother.

H I.
I'M JOZEF THOUGH EVERYONE CALLS ME JOE.

I'm ten now but when I was little I said I wanted to be the pope. Miss Ravanello said that first I'd have to be a priest, then a bishop, then a cardinal and so far no Australian has been the pope. There have only been bishops and cardinals. Our bishop came to St Mary's parish when my brother was confirmed. I asked him what it's like to be a bishop and he said he liked it. I asked Father Barry if he'd ever be a bishop and he said he didn't think so. I was talking to Father Barry after Kim Starling and I helped him at Benediction. I like Benediction with all the incense and candles and flowers and the light shining through the stained glass. I told Miss Ravanello and she said that when she was little Benediction was her favourite thing at church. I also like the singing.

This is Benediction. Mrs Azzopardi helped me with the names of the things.

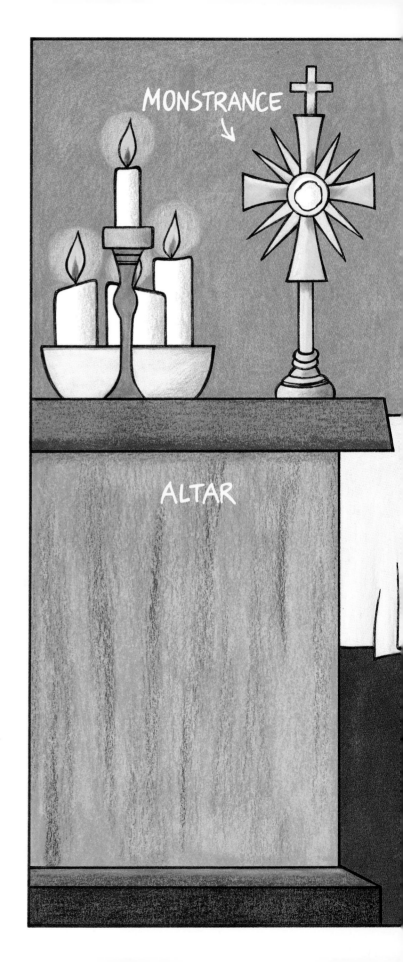

I AM EMILY AND I'M A CATHOLIC.

Today I feel sad. I live with my mother and my sister Jenny. My dad lives down the coast. I often feel sad when I think about it because I wish he would live with us. When I'm feeling sad I sometimes wonder if God really loves us so I asked Mum and she said that God loves us no matter what. I still find it hard to understand.

My best friend is Philomena Fernandes. She came here from Sri Lanka and I call her Philo. When I am at her place her mother cooks curry that makes my mouth and nose tingle. Philo said that in Sri Lanka most of the people are Buddhists but there are quite a lot of Christians and a lot of them are Catholics. When I'm grown up I'd like to go to Sri Lanka. I am learning to cook from my mother so that when I do I can cook them something Australian. I can already make chocolate crackles.

This is Philo and me making chocolate crackles.

MY NAME IS FLAVIO RONCALI AND I'M A CATHOLIC.

My mother helps at the church. She gives Communion out at Mass nearly every Sunday. She also visits some of the sick people. 'I take Jesus to them, Flavio', she told me. There was a pope called Angelo Roncali but he was not related to me though Mum says if I end up like him I'll be doing very well.

Because my grandparents came from Italy we sometimes go to the Italian Mass. Father Adriano, the Italian priest, showed me a photo of himself when he first became a priest. 'This is me when I was ordained', he said. 'Holy Orders is another name for it.'

Priests wore different clothes then. Our priest is Father Barry and he has a border collie dog called Dominic because he is black and white.

This is my mother giving Communion to Mr. Lahoud.
Communion is when Jesus comes to us in a special way. Usually it's at Mass but for sick people it is different.

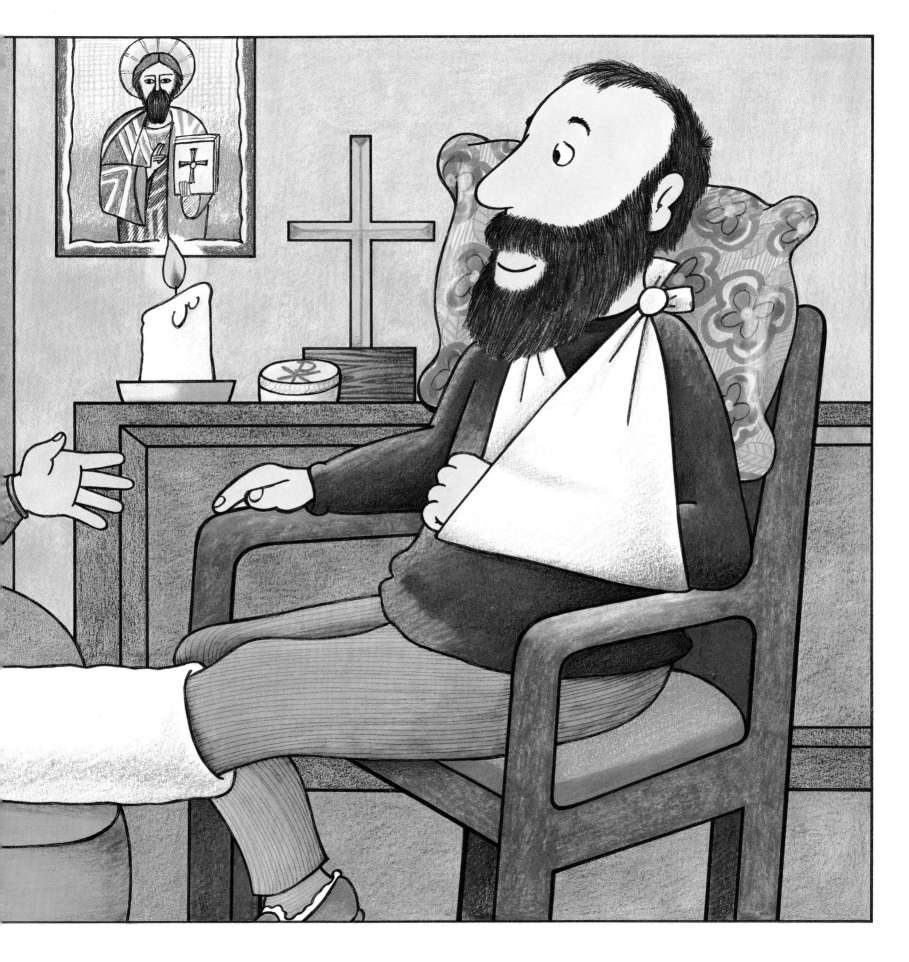

MY NAME IS ZOFIA AND I'M A CATHOLIC.

My grandfather is Polish and on Sundays he and Bobska go off to the Polish Mass because they like to meet their friends and so they can speak Polish. I really like to go to the Polish church for midnight Mass at Christmas when they sing all the old hymns and then we go to stay at Tut and Bobska's house for Christmas dinner.

My little sister Justyna is making her first Communion this year. In our parish when you make your first Communion you do it with your family and you wear your best clothes. When my mother was in grade two all the girls were dressed in white with a veil. And my father says that he had to wear shorts and long socks and a sash! People did some funny things in the old days.

This is a photo of my mother and her cousin when they made their first Communion.

I'M A CATHOLIC AND MY NAME IS ALICE.

I haven't always lived here in St Mary's parish. My father and Mum came from South Australia. My family have lived in Australia for a very long time because we are Kooris, though one of my great-grandfathers was from Scotland and another one was Irish. I am not sure when my family became Catholics. I like being a Catholic and I like being Koori, too. One of the best days to be a Koori was when we all met together the day the ships came into Sydney harbour for the 1988 bicentenary. We carried the Koori flag and I felt that all the people together were my friends. Sometimes I feel like that at Mass but not all the time. My dad says that if we are fair dinkum Catholics we would treat all the people as if they were our friends, like that day walking down the street on Australia Day.
I think that's what God wants.

I'M JULIE LAHOUD AND I'M A CATHOLIC.

In 1928 my great-grandfather came to Australia from Lebanon. He's dead now. My pop's still alive and my grandma. Pop has been sick and he's still going in to the Mercy Hospital every week. Some of the nurses there are nuns. Grandma told me that when she was little nearly all of the nurses at the Catholic hospitals were nuns and that they wore clothes really different from now. She has some photos of them.

I'm a Melkite Catholic. In the really olden days, even before 1928, most Catholics in Australia were from Ireland. In some ways Melkite Catholics are different from Western Catholics but they are mostly the same.

My mum's name is Bernadette and it used to be Bernadette O'Reilly. That's a really Irish name Dad says. Mum said that when she was at school most of the girls had names like hers. Things have really changed. When Australia gets its own saints the first one will be a nun, Sister Mary MacKillop, but I don't think she taught my mother.

One day we went to the hospital to see Pop and some of the sisters were dressed in old-fashioned clothes for the fête. One of them looked like this.

I'M PATRICK AND I'M A CATHOLIC.

I go to St Mary's school but I didn't start school here. I started at Our Lady of Lourdes. At that school our teacher Mr Taylor taught us the 'Hail Mary' and 'The Sign of the Cross'. When I came to St Mary's they knew them here too and I was surprised. Then I found out that no matter where you go there are a whole lot of prayers and other things that Catholics do the same. Miss Ravanello said that 'The Lord's Prayer' is known by all Christians and we can say it together. I told that to my sister, Kerry, who's in year ten and she told me that some of the prayers in the Bible are said by all Christians and all Jews. I asked her about the Jews and she said that Jesus was a Jew and our religion is related to the Jews. Maybe we are cousins. My grandparents came from Ireland and that's one of the reasons I am called Patrick. Another reason is that I was born on March 17 which is St Patrick's Day.

Miss Ravanello got us to do a drawing of ourselves for our religion lesson so I drew myself making the sign of the cross.

17 MARCH ST. PATRICK'S DAY my birthday!

Me making
the sign
of the
cross

Patrick

HELLO, I'M ANDREW AND I'M TEN AND A HALF AND I'M A CATHOLIC.

The other day when I was at Nan's she got her photo album out and we were looking at the photos of when Mum was at school. She had a photo of my uncle Tim when he was an altar boy and one of Mum when she was in the Children of Mary. Nan said that when Mum was little and before that when Nan was little there were all sorts of clubs and things for Catholics to be in. Nan was in the netball team for the Catholic Youth Club. That's where she met Pop. He played football there. Girls wore much longer dresses for netball in those days. Miss Ravanello looks really different in her netball dress. I said to Nan that I thought lots of things had changed. She said yes but it's still our church.

First Published by Collins Dove
A Division of HarperCollins*Publishers* (Australia) Pty Ltd
22-24 Joseph Street
North Blackburn, Victoria 3130

First published 1992
Designed by William Hung
Cover design by William Hung
Cover illustration Marjory Gardner
Text by Graham English
Typeset in Pilgrim and Perpetua by EMS Typesetting Pty Ltd

ISBN 0-8146-2061-2.